PIRENE'S FOUNTAIN

PIRENE'S FOUNTAIN

Senior Editor	Lark Vernon Timmons
Submissions and Review Editor	Elizabeth Nichols, CA
Design & Layout Editor	Steve Asmussen
Associate Editors	Royce Hamel
	Linda E. Kim
	Paul Kim
	Kelly Cressio-Moeller
Web Editor	Katherine Herschler
Art Consultant	Tracy McQueen
Editor & Publisher	Ami Kaye

Pirene's Fountain
Culinary Poems

Volume 12, Issue 20

Pirene's Fountain: A Journal of Poetry
Volume 12, Issue 20
Copyright © 2019 Pirene's Fountain
Paperback ISSN 2331-1096

Layout, Book & Cover Design: Steven Asmussen
Copyediting: Elizabeth Nichols, CA & Linda E. Kim
Cover Artist: © Mustipan - Dreamstime.com

All rights reserved: except for the purpose of quoting brief passages for review, no part of this book may be reproduced or transmitted in any form or by any means, electronic or mechanical, including photocopying, recording, or by any information storage and retrieval system, without permission in writing from the publisher.

Glass Lyre Press, LLC
P.O. Box 2693
Glenview, IL 60025

www.GlassLyrePress.com

Contents

Poetry

Shanta Acharya
    Coconut Milk   13

Rita Anderson
    Flour   14

Ruth Bavetta
    Song for My Refrigerator   16

Daisy Bassen
    Sonnet à la Mode   17

Margo Berdeshevsky
    News From the Garden…   18

J.P. Dancing Bear
    By the Light of the Lemon   20

Yoko Danno
    Bosom-Stone Cuisine: 21

Lori Desrosiers
    Cheese   24

Alicia Elkort
    I Woke to the Scent Of Roasting Coffee   25

Susan Fox
    Quailbone   26

Diane Frank
    Pheasant   27

Cynthia Gallaher
    May You Have Salty Days Ahead   28

Jane Hirshfield
    Da Capo   31
    Milk   32
    Wine Grapes for Breakfast   34

Carol Levin
    Cantaloupe Deities   35

Cameron Morse
    Hamburgers   36

Robbi Nester
    Three Star Chef   37

Joey Nicoletti
    The Difference Between Prosciutto and Speck   38

Connie Post
    Rupture   39
Jeannie E. Roberts
    Oyster   40
Claire D. Roof
    The Batter   42
Claudia Serea
    Ode to Slow Cooking   43
Neil Silberblatt
    Butternut Squash Atonement – A Recipe   45
Kalpna Singh-Chitnis
    Tripitaka   47
Tim Suermondt
    The Breakfast Before Leaving   48
Maria Terrone
    Stripping the Pear   49

Reviews

Against Prompts by Bill Yarrow   53
Arabesque by Rachel Dacus   59
The Practicing Poet by Diane Lockward   63
Narrow Bridge by Robbi Nester   67

Publication Credits

Contributor Notes

POETRY

Coconut Milk

Shanta Acharya

My basket was heavy with shopping,
but the coconut milk was missing.

Sainsbury's did not have the ready-to-cook
variety, made in Thailand –
creamy as full-fat milk and just as silky.

Will this do? The shop assistant with a kind, withered
face handed me a solid cake of coconut milk.
I smiled, surprised. He smiled, shuffled off, satisfied.

That evening I cook the prawns
with finely chopped onions, mushrooms, tomatoes,
stirring in slivers of coconut milk.
The flavours waft through open windows into the sunset.

Moving to the rhythm of old Hindi film songs
you loved to hear, I savour your presence, father.

The sun retires behind trees,
swaying to the raga and rasa of life –

teaching me that like the sun, moon and stars
you are always there, though briefly revealed.
When our paths diverge we must let go.

Sprinkling freshly chopped coriander leaves,
ground garlic and crushed chilli on the simmering curry,
my eyes are blinded with grief and a child's fury.

FLOUR

Rita Anderson

I'm up to my elbows
I haven't made this
Not like you used to
Three pizzas, six children
One meal, no leftover
I never had a family like that
One son, grown and flown
From the ground up
From scratch Hot tap
water revives dry yeast
Just like this action
activates memory, a child-
hood dropped in a box
Cover with a clean towel
For hours, let it rise
It's been years
My own silver bowls, now
You only had one
My hands, now, look like
Your hands then
But even with adult hands
They don't make or bake
Flawlessly like you did
Mother, flour queen
After all these years
What made me dig
out your recipe?
Because I haven't seen you
Nothing like I remember
Now, in a wheelchair
with a nurse attending
When is the last time you baked?
So I'm in a flurry
To bury the lonely
Flour on the floor

The counter, my hair
In the air as I pound
Dough into pans
Unsure, my hands never
For better for worse
Became your hands

Song for My Refrigerator

Ruth Bavetta

Praise for the pomegranate hidden
back of the butter. Sing psalms
of joy for the orange juice
and kugel. Wake with the sun
and cherry red radishes. Let us
remember lettuce, celery and peas.

Make a pour of cold milk
the point of the cereal. Dream
of cherry pie with whipped cream
tonight. Listen for the purr
of cool in the making, spreading
its fingers around all that's within.

Sing for your breakfast, for all
starry mornings, for wind in the trees,
and seagulls at sea. Listen for children
clinking their lunchboxes, wish
them a day without rifles and pain.

Sonnet à la Mode

Daisy Bassen

If I'd spent the morning making a pie,
I'd have a pie now, gold crust blind-baked,
The apples sandy with sugar, loose.
I'd take the knife in my right hand
To cut:
The slice uneven, louche,
Syrup tart on the blade.
The first mouthful is the best, swallowing
The heady scents that filled the early hours:
The suggestion of ultimate satisfaction,
Humming, my lips around the tines.
When I finished, there'd be no evidence,
Every dish washed and dried, stacked.
There'd be no butter left in the house, no cream.

News from the Garden...

Margo Berdeshevsky

Her report to all assorted & *Zen*:
Better color. Better lungs. New
bracelets & painted toes.

Announcement of improvements to her mind,
now she likes her sliced *canard* well done, her
potager-picked raspberries tongue-stain ripe,

her *haut-médoc* goblet brimmed & summer
temperate, her *lentilles de Puy*, curried, spiced
as the night heat teases & rises

but most — she's always hungry now, famished
for still another bowl   of country air —
Gorging all week & nude & morning eager,

here where the red fox-pup on his haunches
watches, twitch-hides under his chosen weeping
willow that shades its lotus pond,   & she nears

& he eyes her barefoot steps, his
gaze keen as a morning bread knife.
He scuttles back between mare-high

stalks of cattle maize & whispers to tell his mama
of a blonde *femme* there — in morning's shadows,
there — naked as Poussin's *Nurture of Bacchus!*

Safe in the stalks, he surveys.
Better to be crouching than too well seen
by that blonde still lapping her bowl

of country coffee with honey. He's a fox
after all, pepper-red as Mars moving into middle
August skies surrounded by the Perseids.

Vines against the farmhouse twine in country
morning sex, and bees, all day & all night in riots of
alleluia choruses climb the lime tree beside the pear.

To the unseen waiting fox and to all assorted & *Zen*,
this news: the blonde's well-fed and naked sighs, her
whispered soft as a waiting kiss *amen* ....

Where night skies whisk lightening, where
promises of thunder, a gibbous moon & sunrise
ready for tastes of breakfast, too — the pear

will press against her French wall, all womanly,
& the fox's ever nude blonde will feast & feast
on nature's plate, will grow fat on bowls of eager

air—&— this is all for
this day's news.
If there is more— Just wait.

By the Light of the Lemon

J.P. Dancing Bear
for Ami Kaye

even the moon is envious of the light of the lit-up lemon: its leaves turning into dancers: pirouette and plié like they are caught by the wind: small seeds replacing the stars: lemon-light unleashed in the night: and all you can think of is the taste on your tongue: you prepare the subtlest spices to compliment: already imagining the citrus sliced: baked over the naked sides of fish: tangy and sweet juice to stir: adding its brilliance: into a sauce: a marinade: no one should mistake your motives: you love this bright moment of yellow: but the lemon is fresh: it would be a terrible waste: if you did not enjoy all of it

BOSOM-STONE CUISINE:

Yoko Danno

Zen monks used to warm themselves

by putting hot stones, near their stomachs,

to ward off hunger,

hence the frugal meal at tea ceremony

*

One Soup

It has been blowing all night;

your face reflected

in the clear soup

is mingled with sea weed

in the black-lacquered

bowl

*

Three Side Dishes

i

This side dish sashimi is to be put

on the far side of your meal tray;

how the table may be turned

is anybody's guess;

you'd better eat the staple food first,

boiled rice and pickles,

just in case

ii

Your tongue won't be burnt

if you eat these simmered vegetables,

carrot, daikon and butterbur flower-buds,

three gentle musketeers

on a special service to entertain you

in a ceramic bowl

with a lid

iii

Which meat is sizzling

on the hot plate, you may wonder,

this is just tofu skewered,

roasted over charcoal,

coated with citrus-flavored miso

like a soft futon

CHEESE

Lori Desrosiers

Cheese: noun. 1. A substance born of milk or cream due to ~~magic~~ the addition of rennet and chemical reaction. 2. My grandfather Jack's generosity embodied in how he spread the cream cheese on the bagels. *Schmear*. 3. Bread becomes divine by grilling, slathering, placing gently on a cracker. 4. Every town in France has its own cheese. Walk into a *charcuterie* and find the wheel of it placed reverently on a large cutting board. Ask for a taste. Your life changes in this moment. 5. Melted: Brie, Cheddar, Swiss, Chevre, oh God, chevre. 6. My daughters would choose cheese over candy every time. Even chocolate. 7. Chocolate with cheese. Seriously, try it. 8. Mixed cheeses, infused with peppers, dill, strawberries, herbs. 9. Sliced with bologna, pepperoni, salami. 10. Melted mozzarella: pizza, calzone, lasagna, parmesan, ricotta. Italian orgasm.

I Woke to the Scent of Roasting Coffee

Alicia Elkort

a regular occurrence of my childhood. My father would wake before sunup, lay
the beans across a dimpled pan, put the oven on low. When the beans were done,

he'd grind them to powder then brew, the sound of water filling a glass pitcher
traveling to my bedroom, the acrid scent of roasting beans, the high-pitched

whirling of the grinder awakening me, now peevish at my father's insistence
on a perfect cup of java. Some mornings I'd find flats of strawberries

from the wholesale market downtown or bundles of flowers, or my father elbow
deep making poppy and sesame bagels. Other times it was salt-water taffy

or, one snowy morning when living in Fairbanks, the beginning of a ginger-bread
house made entirely from scratch, patterns of a wall, a chimney, a door scattered

across the kitchen table. But the coffee ritual patterned my awareness, long
before any of the myriad coffee shops that today mark my city's landscape.

I woke to the scent of roasting coffee, four months after my father died,
but there was no roasting coffee, only a quiver of its merciful scent.

QUAILBONE

Susan Fox

I give you the wishbone of a quail
not for wishing
only to hold.
No wish is as frail
as these ivory pins,
this tiny ogive with its fluted hinge.
Wishes are brutal.
Why shatter this splinter
inchspan
this wake of a seed —
for what desire?
Seedwake   dreamprow
only to hold
for its memory of wings,
of dense sweet meat.

PHEASANT

Diane Frank

It was the most sensual meal I had ever eaten. Roadkill pheasant. "Joanne has a really good nose," Joya explained. "She can tell if the meat is fresh. Just a few minutes before we found it, the pheasant was still flying."

At the time, I was living in a small university town in Iowa – not always easy for someone from San Francisco. Joanne and Joya were people I could be myself with, and vice versa. They loved birds, and if they found a hawk, an eagle, or a pheasant dead by the side of the road, they'd pull over, honor the bird, pluck the feathers, and use them for a headdress or a ceremonial shield.

More food in that bird than two people could eat, so Joanne and Joya invited me to dinner before my evening class. They lit the table with candles and filled their rose-colored vintage glass plates with pheasant, stuffing, sweet potatoes, brussels sprouts and cranberry sauce. An early Thanksgiving. Everything smelled like the most delicious incense. Everything tasted like ambrosia. Before that night, I did not know food could put you in an altered state of consciousness. It was really hard to leave that table when it was time to teach my evening class, even though it was poetry.

Rainbow bird flies home.
Blessed, filled with light, to open sky.
Honor the feathers.

May You Have Salty Days Ahead

Cynthia Gallaher

to sit in the heavily wooded Appalachians,
it's hard to imagine remnants of Iapetus Ocean,

300 feet beneath us,
filled with 600 million year-old brine,

saturated juice of amniotic fluid,
blood plasma, lymphatic circulation,

starter liquid of worldwide
nation states,

the sea-like soup we swim in,
mineral springs from which we stir.

historically, too little of it,
now too much, a modern profusion.

"restricting salt is about as easy
as cutting back on blinking," one M.D. said.

yet ancients' lack thereof
often meant annihilation.

upon again reaching the outskirts
of civilized life sometime in the future,

might salt be worth more than books or gold?
we raise gardens, we butcher meat,

we tap water from the deep,
but without salt from far-flung locales

would life as we know it, change,
starting with the gentle stanch of salty kisses.

would we mourn the Cyprus black of pyramid shapes,
the Galos salt caves of Krakow,

the Celtic grey of Irish seas
launching unseen fireworks in our mouths,

the Egyptian knack for preserving mummies,
the Mexican offerings at the *ofrenda*,

rites of purification,
disintegration of the dead,

the kosher coarseness of migrations,
Himalayan reds drawn from loftiest rocks,

fleur de sel caviar, salt flowers raked from
great sheets along Atlantic shores,

floating like snowflakes,
smelling of violets.

the easy preservations of olives, cheese,
salami, anchovies, and brining of American turkeys.

could our millennial blood hold steady
at 0.9% salt, dissolving our

fatigue and cranky moods, dancing with water
as a balanced path to rehydration.

oh crystalline structure of
sodium and chloride,

cheap and positively charged,
iconic ions we take for granted,

to be valued at any price
next time we lack.

let's relish the pinch, the dash,
between thumb and forefinger,

the half teaspoon's disappearing
act in boiling water.

the salt grinder's mild cascade
across a platter of vegetables.

sprinkle it lightly through
your days on earth, but may you sprinkle it,

seeding life's highs as well as lows,
where watermelon can become sweeter,
tears more savory.

DA CAPO

Jane Hirshfield

Take the used-up heart like a pebble
and throw it far out.

Soon there is nothing left.
Soon the last ripple exhausts itself
in the weeds.

Returning home, slice carrots, onions, celery.
Glaze them in oil before adding
the lentils, water, and herbs.

Then the roasted chestnuts, a little pepper, the salt.
Finish with goat cheese and parsley. Eat.
You may do this, I tell you, it is permitted.
Begin again the story of your life.

MILK

Jane Hirshfield

From time to time the placid
shrugs its shoulders—
earthquakes, for instance—

but still the world
depends
on placid things' resistance.

The fire requires
its trees,
the sea its hem of boulders,

the wind
without its halls
would howl in silence;

for everything that
flares up, something lowers
itself, digs in

for an existence
in the long haul, slows.
It may well be the placid knows

its worth. The cow whose
calf was taken
eats again—but do not guess

too quickly at the meaning
in the red hips' unbent squareness,
the large-jawed head

half-buried in the grass:
with each fly's weightless
bite, the thick skin shivers.

The placid, unlike us,
lives in the moment.
Something must;

like chairs,
or painted dressers,
on an earth where loss

is so all present
that we drink it without thinking,
blue-white in its early morning glass.

Wine Grapes for Breakfast

Jane Hirshfield

Sweet
at first
on the tongue,
hours later
the red grapes
still sting,
as if trying
to tell me something—
what the hook
tells the fish
perhaps,
or the wand
or stick hears
before conductor
or mule driver
brings it down.

Cantaloupe Deities

Carol Levin

Just as your babushkaed grandmother
performed her final test in her time

the tip of your thumb probes
inspecting a spongy spot.

You nuzzle your nose to the webby
ridges of the fruit expecting

fragrance will exude secrets.

All of this you perform carefully
covertly watching husbands

filling grocery carts incandescent
under a vast ceiling of lights like a maze

of planets magnetizing pyramids of melons.

Later in the dark you slice
moist halves onto plates. Clean away

pulp, uncover heart meat, sweet
at the exact spot

you'd tenderly fingered. You knew

what would happen.
You close your eyes, take

the fruit into your mouth:
goddess of the sun

swallowing the god of sky.

HAMBURGERS

Cameron Morse

When you call because you've fallen
cleaning the bathroom at the Montessori
Children's House of Blue Springs,

I'm patting hamburgers in the kitchen,
weighing cold clumps of ground beef
on your silver scale, pressing
red meat onto wax paper with the heel

of my hand. Red squiggles dangle
from my lifeline. When I see the missed
call and seven messages, I dial
the nurse and sit down on the front step

to wait for your car to round the corner.
I wait to count the fetal movements, smearing
your lower abdomen with cow blood,
and say everything's going to be all right.

Three Star Chef

Robbi Nester

It's all in the gesture, in the way
he tosses the salt, overhand,
into the soup, or crimps the edges
of the pastry dough.
He never writes down recipes,
a stalk of rosemary tucked
behind his ear, lifting the beets
so tenderly out of the earth,
still bearded with roots.
He tilts his head, steps
slowly, as though to music.
His vision is contagious.
As he turns to walk up
the path, I see a faint rainbow
arc over the farmhouse
like a cloche. Anything
done with intention becomes
a form of art, of prayer.

The Difference Between Prosciutto and Speck

Joey Nicoletti

is in the amount of flavor
provided by the fat,
as my friend Jeff tells me.
"That difference is everything,

like Pluto not being a planet anymore,
because it's too small,
as opposed to Mars and the stars
out tonight. Let's eat."

We dig in. We chomp
our sumptuous feast
of these thin
slices of meat, salty,

glittering on wide,
vermilion plates,
beneath a round, candlelit
picnic table of sky.

RUPTURE

Connie Post

Someone cracks an egg in a bowl
and the world is broken

a silver fork ruptures the yolk,
and the sea is never whole again

an omelette is made
the egg loses itself
among the butter and onion
and shredded cheese

but when it is folded over
just before it leaves the pan
the chef notices something
about the brown edges
—the soft way a crust forms

sooner than expected
everything slides onto a white plate
and the table genuflects

as morning passes
there may be small ways
we remember the shell
times we shudder at the sound
of shattering

but even after the pan
is removed from an open flame
we find graceful ways
to slide out of a room
step over a fractured equator

and clean our plates
in a small kitchen
with no running water

OYSTER

Jeannie E. Roberts

You drop and slide
within silken tides
of eternity
slipping
between now and soon
swirling
through past and future
joining jelly fish
as it rises   then falls away

You could hold
the oldest pearl
the youngest seed
as you filter
then feed on plankton
but you've been caught

O how they crave
your mass of brine-softness
your primordial kiss   where
you clasp and clench
your jewel-prone chest
only   to be opened

O sea-swept *Bivalvia*
how you glow
on the half-shell
gleam
steeped in sauce   when
you're swallowed

You drop and slide
within silken tides
of eternity
slipping

between now and soon
swirling
through past and future
joining belly's dish
as it rises   then falls away

THE BATTER

Claire D. Roof

Cream the yellow burst butter with the white sugar and then the brown.
Use the wooden spoon your mother left you in 1995.
Watch the windows for lightning to strike your hands as they work.

Crack open the eggs with your sorrow.
Blend them with your broken winged heart.
Utter your wounded words over the bowl.

In a separate slightly worn out bowl, add the dry tears you cannot cry.
Add baking soda and salt into your wounds that settle in your mourning space.
Pre-heat the oven with all that brings you solace.

Add the white all purpose flour slowly with your lost lust.
Tablespoon by tablespoon, blend your curses into the cookie dough.
Sprinkle the dark chocolate chips into your jagged blue soul.

Spray your cookie sheet with love's memories.
Drop by tablespoons the batter of your loss.
Try not to burn the lonely house of your hurt down.

Taste the bitterness of dark chocolate chips.
Swallow the comfort of your baking.
Share your sorrow in the sweetness you have created as your own.

Start again.
Carry the recipe in your fragile heart pocket.
Remind yourself to live and taste the world anew.

ODE TO SLOW COOKING

Claudia Serea

Nothing good comes quickly,
the old woman said,
chopping the Holy Trinity
for the pan.

Rushing never made a great stew.

You have to let the parsnip fibers break
and the vertebrae sing.

Let the marrow melt
and dissolve, slowly,
the way water carves limestone
into caves.

Add the ox heart tomatoes later,
and feel the sweetness
when you taste for salt.

Think how far, how long
the peppercorns traveled
from Vietnam
and the Malabar Coast
only to open their small eyes
in your pot.

Add bay leaves,
the chef's Olympian crown.

Pour a swirl of wine
and taste again
the dark nipples of the grapes
in the seaside wind.

History is there,
and love

with a hint of grass
in the lamb bone.

Butternut Squash Atonement – A Recipe

Neil Silberblatt

In the beginning was the Word,
and the Word was
butter - unsalted, cream butter -
not Fleishman's or Imperial,
not "I can't believe" - although
I don't
any longer.
Just enough to hide the wrapper
from my mom,
who would ask,
who – in her 95 years - never ate milk with meat,
knowingly.

Into this sinful butter
is cast chopped celery and onions
and whole garlic cloves (2 or 3),
cooked until the celery is soft,
the onion translucent,
and the mixture smells of home.

Now, chicken stock is added (4 cups).
Kosher for my mom,
who would ask,
who - in her 95 years - never ate non-Kosher meat
lest her entry be barred in Gan Ayden[1].

Into this comes butternut or winter squash
roasted until smooth and mashed
until resembling the color of
the clay of her Kishinev shtetl.
Then, savory and rosemary –
burlesque strippers –
who tease the flavor out of this soup.

At the very end, cream is added.
Non-dairy, for my mom,
who would ask,
and fresh-grated nutmeg.

Once, by mistake, I used real cream
and lied to her.
How she loved the taste of that soup.
How she forgave the lie,
asking for seconds.

Oh, do not cast her from Paradise
on account of that tainted soup.
Let the sin be on me
and the sweet taste be on her lips
for eternity.

[1]: Garden of Eden or Paradise

TRIPITAKA*

Kalpna Singh-Chitnis

In the three baskets, there were meals
enough to serve everyone.

In the three baskets, there were the offerings
for the past, present, and future.

From the three baskets, they ate,
not to be hungry in lifetimes.

From the three baskets, they learned
how to cook and serve the universe.

In the three baskets, they saw
the sun, moon, and stars dwelling.

In the three baskets, they discovered
the mountains, rivers, and green fields.

In the three baskets, the rain poured incessantly
for everyone thirsty on earth.

In the three baskets, they found
the recipes of *Nirvana*, written and unwritten.

---

*: Tripitaka (the three bamboo baskets) is the collected discourses of the Buddha, written in the Pali language.

The Breakfast Before Leaving

Tim Suermondt

I stir the cornflakes and the coffee
with the same spoon—am I actually
leaving this house, never to return?

In minutes I will be out in the world,
armadilloed with memory and the hope
that the future will treat me fairly.

I lift the bowl to my lips, suck up
the last drop of milk and the last stubborn
cornflake—and say hello to my ghost

standing at the bottom of the stairs, younger
than I am, but not by much. He says he'll
take care of things here, make sure

the new owners comport themselves well,
better than I ever did—I watch him climb
the dusty steps, not halting to say bon voyage.

Stripping the Pear

Maria Terrone

Their heart-shaped bottoms sway
in the fan's gentle nudging—
yesterday's golden girls bruised
and woozy in a dance hall's wee hours.
Nearly joined at the hip, they shape
a parenthesis—always an afterthought,
chosen by default. Mottled brown
from time and neglect, they wave
their stems like flags, reliving the days
they swung from branch-tips,
felt the power of their swelling weight.
I consider banishing them from sight
but instead, choose the one most scarred
and test-peel away an inch of blotchy skin:
honey leaps to my nose and throat.
I strip the pear naked and split it in two.
Nectar flows from smooth, moist flesh
as I carve out the buried seeds
of rebirth, its bridal-white flowering.

REVIEWS

AGAINST PROMPTS
by Bill Yarrow

REVIEWED BY ELIZABETH NICHOLS, CA

Bill Yarrow

The late social critic and comedian George Carlin remarked, "It isn't fair: the caterpillar does all the work, and the butterfly gets all the glory." In *Against Prompts,* Bill Yarrow—perhaps the George Carlin of poets—delivers an acerbic manifesto decrying the use of prompts in the craft of poetry. He champions the industrious caterpillar, the creator of the chrysalis from its own body, the "real poet [that] designs and builds a livable space and makes it elegant and beautiful… designs and builds, board by board, brick by brick, what [it] imagines" (134). Yarrow, like Carlin, has no respect for glory thieves—for those poet-butterflies that glue chitin and "flesh to the bones of someone else's skeleton" (133). *Against Prompts* calls out the "creative-writing teachers and professional…writers" that rely on prompts: rely on "others to tell them what to write" (134). Yarrow's manifesto also uses biting, beautiful imagery and word play to critique the business of poetry: publishing, submissions, and even back-cover blurbs. *Against Prompts* pushes back against the fast-food-like convenience of poetry prompts through Yarrow's sharp, playful poetry. Perhaps Yarrow is at his most Carlin-esque when he bites out, "Prompts are the cancer of creativity: they metastasize shit." *Against Prompts* is a deft work that unequivocally proves that cutting out the cancer of prompts produces powerful, impactful poetry that is sui generis.

Each chapter title in *Against Prompts* commands the poet to look inward for inspiration. Yarrow, in essence, is telling the poet to "Be Heuristic," hubristic, ekphrastic, sadistic, forensic, ballistic, acoustic, and linguistic. He is demanding that the poet turns away from inane prompts and instead draw from his or her own creative wellspring. "Why do you need someone **outside yourself** telling you what to write about?" Asks Yarrow in his manifesto. "Have you no inner resources? Have you no self-respect?" (134) Several poems in *Against Prompts* refer to Yarrow's critical questions. In "End Game," Yarrow equates the poet himself as the poetry. In other words, the life of the poet becomes his poetry and therefore the two are indistinguishable. Here, life does not merely imitate art, but becomes art:

from "END GAME"

We are the past story, the present story,
and also the new story, the future story.
We end as stanza ends, as a chapter ends.
Our book is not long—it is just endless.

 Blake said

   One thought fills immensity

 I say, one person fills eternity. (27)

  Similarly, in "THE MIRROR TIRES OF LOOKING AT ITSELF," Yarrow reminds the poet of Whitman's famous maxim: he contains multitudes. "We are all essays," proclaims the poem's speaker, "some poorly written, / some sparkling prose. The best of us / has a thesis, a goal which organizes / our lives. We prove claims / as we go. Transitions are our friends" (83). In the final stanza, the speaker asks a series of questions not unlike Yarrow's in his manifesto. Each question asks what the inner life of a druggist, dry cleaner, barista, etc., would look like, would feel like. The speaker directly addresses the poet in the final two lines: "Have you asked the butcher's daughter? / Have you approached the neighborhood fellatrice?" (83) Here, Yarrow parallels his manifesto: "Are you a real poet or just a house painter? Are you a real poet or just a tuck pointer? Are you a real poet or just a squatter?" (134) A real poet, in other words, does not need the blueprints—the prompt—from an architect; the real poet is the architect. There is no need for prompt; all the poet needs is his imagination for inspiration. In the case of "THE MIRROR TIRES OF LOOKING AT ITSELF," the poet imagines the inner lives of those around him.

  Yarrow's paronomasias (the witty exploitation of the meaning and ambiguity of words) underscores the ineffectual nature of poetry prompts. "Today," explains Yarrow, "prompts rush in to fill the vacuum of a tired writer's lack of imagination or paucity of ideas. Today, soi-disant writers on social media post things like 'I don't know what to write about. Could someone give me a prompt?' I'm saddened by the wretchedness of such pleas" (134). Yarrow's sometimes experimental poems stand as proof of the pointlessness of prompts. They demonstrate that the wealth of the poet's own imagination, of language, and of life is truly inexhaustible. In "8 NEWS WAYS OF LOOKING AT WAFFLES," Yarrow is playfully tongue-in-cheek, pairing normally contemplative concepts with the image of a breakfast food. In doing so, Yarrow forces the reader, and practicing poets, to juxtapose two seemingly disparate subjects to create meaning.

8 NEWS WAYS OF LOOKING AT WAFFLES

1. the mind (in its righteousness)
waffles

2. the conscience (in its scrupulousness)
Waffles

3. the heart (in its cupidity)
waffles

4. the soul (in its annihilation)
waffles

5. the tongue (in its appeasement)
waffles

6. the skin (in its lethargy)
waffles

7. the body (in its luxury)
waffles

8. life (in its delirium)
waffles

Yarrow also manipulates line, stanza, and repetition to upset expectations and create meaning in his poems. In "THE SEPARATION," lines jut left and right, scattering across the page. It is as if the images come to the reader in *bokeh*, and only stepping back to look at the whole produces a connected, pointillistic poem. As in "8 WAYS TO LOOK AT WAFFLES," in "THE SEPARATION" Yarrow also places discordant images next to each other: "I pondered Yeats / I pondered my heart / I pondered my past / I pondered my children / I pondered my marriage. / I pondered my future / I concluded / life is rich / pudding / life is rough / soup" (82). The surrealistic food similies are echoed in "PAR DELICATESSE;" the speaker declares, "My life? / A shmere in a foreign appetite" (18). In *Against Prompts*, Yarrow puts his command of poetry and language on full display. His work is the exemplar of his manifesto. His chapbook leaves the poet, the writer, the student asking, "Why use prompts as a crutch when there is an unlimited universe of poetic possibility in the imagination, in life?"

An obvious critique of Yarrow's manifesto is that countless poets past used a celebrated canon as a catalyst for their own work. The A.D. Finch poem "Coy Mistress," a response to Andrew Marvell's metaphysical poem "To His Coy Mistress," is one such famous example. But, Yarrow anticipates this critique in his manifesto. "I am well aware," he expounds, "that writers in previous centuries wrote on certain subjects at the behest of patrons, as a result of challenges, and on the occasion or anniversary of certain events. Those may be provocations to creative invention, but they are not prompts in the modern sense of the term" (134). Here, Yarrow makes the distinction between the working reality of poets past and contemporary poets' supposed panacea to writer's block in the form of the prompt. This distinction is keenly felt when comparing, for an example, John Donne's poems written for his wealthy friends or patrons and modern poetry prompts such as "…explore other natural occurrences that coincide with summer…and write a poem in tribute to the hottest days of the year" (135). The dissimilitude is inescapable: akin to a handcrafted timepiece versus cheap knock-off. Further, Yarrow highlights poems with titles like "After Yeats," "After Stevens," "After Pound," "After Ginsberg," etc., and lays out their lack of originality: "If you take someone's poem and write your "own" version of that poem… you haven't really written a poem either" (133). While Yarrow himself has a poem whose subtitle is "after Walt Whitman," his ensuing lines do not directly pattern themselves on Whitman's. Instead, "SONG OF UNSELF" falls into the tradition of A.D. Finch's aforementioned response to Marvell's work:

SONG OF UNSELF

> I celebrate myself and singe myself
> and what you illume, I refuse
> for every Adam betrothed to you will me betray
>
> I chafe and incite my soul
> I bake and chafe in my disease
> my speech, every item of tongue foams in this soil-free dust
>
> earth's parents ... whose parents ...
> arrrrggghhh ... I now sixty-seven
> sixty-eight, sixty-nine years
>
> chagrin besmears me, increases
> till death, old shoals in obeisance
>
> nothing suffices as harbor
> but to permit to claw at every yawing chasm
> exuberance is beauty ... lesion of enthusiasm
>
> (Incompetent Translations and Inept Haiku, 194)

Yarrow is in conversation with Whitman and, instead of falling into step with the nature poet, refuses what Whitman "illumes." It is as if Dostoevsky's bitter narrator from *Notes from Underground* is reacting to Whitman's transcendentalist "Song." Hence, instead of taking the skeleton of Whitman's acclaimed poem and re-canning its message into a stale echo, Yarrow offers a counterpoint to Whitman with a potent, discordant voice and message. *Against Prompts* therefore addresses the obvious critique to Yarrow's manifesto by demonstrating the difference between an original, poetic response to another poet's work and the wretched calls of modern poets for prompts.

In the end, while Yarrow forthrightly states that writers who use prompts offend him, he does not advocate for the abolition of prompts altogether. Yarrow elucidates, "At its best, a prompt is analogous to playing scales on the piano—a method possibly to develop facility, necessary perhaps for honing a skill, maybe a way to warm up one's hands, but no one in his or her right mind would pay to see a pianist play scales" (134). Prompts can therefore be used by poets as practice to hone their craft, but they should not be used to write a serious work. As Yarrow concludes, "Thus, let's not pretend any significant work came from a prompt. And let's not pretend any serious writer of the past ever worked from prompts" (134). Importantly, Yarrow does advocate for the abatement of the use of prompts in the classroom, bemoaning lazy professors who tell their students what to write and thus stifle their creativity. If those same students read *Against Prompts,* however, Yarrow need not worry. His manifesto and his work vibrantly and fiercely demonstrate that prompts are a crutch best left behind. In the modern television adaptation *Sherlock* (2010), Sherlock Holmes (Benedict Cumberbatch) reveals to John Watson (Martin Freeman) that he does not need the aluminum crutch he has been using to walk; Watson's old war injury healed long ago. The only crutch that remains is in his mind. In *Against Prompts,* the poetry prompt is an aluminum crutch that cripples creativity and produces only banality. As Yarrow concludes, "If you need a prompt to write, you may as well just give up" (135).

ARABESQUE
by Rachel Dacus

REVIEWED BY LINDA E. KIM

Rachel Dacus' *Arabesque* is an intimate and delicate portrayal of grief, trauma, and resilience. The poet's intuitive hand is seen in all the "spider-silk / connections" she creates between physicality and interiority. The urgent need for motion gives insight into the speaker's psyche. The human inclination to flee and escape pain is deeply relatable, especially when memories haunt us.

Family is the utmost source of pain in a world in which parents abandon children, lovers part, and loving relationships are torn. Crushing anxieties stem from "an ocean of loss." Remembrance becomes a "lifelong flinch / at banged doors, dropped cups, / and sudden, alarming shouts." Terse lineation emphasizes the distortion of memory.

Trauma warps perception itself. Its lingering effects are felt in the speaker's relationships, serving to alienate her from others. In "Everything is Relative," the speaker thinks running is the best coping mechanism left:

> "Einstein's definition of the universe
> was taffy-fluid. So I put on running shoes.
> Everything is my relatives.
> *Relative* to the observer's velocity.
> Maybe if I sprint faster, more space
> will dilate time and distance me
> from them, let me lope ahead of myself
> and break the tape—except that time's
>
> again bending, and I bump into my father,
> once a panther, now a prune in a dish." (70)

The harder the speaker tries to "attain the speed of forgetfulness," the more futile the effort seems. Always there is the creeping worry that there is no escape. Anxiety coils and unfurls in bewildering arabesque patterns that disorientate. The mind becomes a trap, a Möbius strip, an unending infinity fraught with worry. "The pull of time and space to my origins / is a black hole now."

But "Motion was remedy." The speaker still needs to try.

> I crave the loneliness to spite it, the kind
> that makes my feet hungry for new miles.

Yet willful independence is still isolation. Disconnecting from others is not the solution to living. Pretending otherwise betrays a desperation that nips at the heels. Trying to forget the past by willfully running from it, to deny it ever existed, is a learned defense that stagnates growth and stifles healing. Avidly pretending trauma does not exist leads to a crippling fear of ever breathing life into memory.

In *Arabesque*, it does not take long for fear of memory to transform into bitter anger instead. The last remnants of a loving relationship can be seen in the ripped photographs and torn up letters falling as "arabesques / of calligraphy. Crinkled hurts / spiraled into the bin. / Even without paper, we wrote / furiously for years of blame."

So bitter are these wounds, so poisonously do they linger, that proud isolation begets self-destruction once the last artifices of love are obliterated:

> We must make mulch
> of the pulp, learn new scripts,
> clean the shadows of our erasures,
> and virgin our leaves
> with ruthless forgetting.

A ruthlessly insecure avoidance of the past does not teach the speaker how to confront, carry, and reconcile with her inner turmoil. In scouring the past of all vestiges of pain, the speaker has instead become more fragile, less resilient, more vulnerable.

Yet in destruction there is also room for resurrection. Creation is a "deceptive work that seems like destruction / but is really a building out of the elements / of dissolving an old form / into a lighter vessel to launch." And ballet is a composition of movements, poses, arabesques.

It starts with the extension of the back leg, the positioning of the dancer's hands in the air. An arabesque is a statement of ballet's tight control of the self. The artist remade, reborn, into the very picture of grace under pressure. Behind the apparent ease of the arabesque is the sheer strength it takes to keep the stomach firm, the supporting leg grounded, the back leg extended in airborne poses. A steadiness is required both physically and psychologically.

But fragility does not make for solid ground.

What betrays the facade of perfection is the fine tremor of muscles, the strain of ligaments, the teeth gritting agony of broken bones and spinal cord injuries. Worse, acrid self-doubt begins to besiege the mind:

> Perched on one leg I kissed the floor,
> toe pointing to heaven, Tchaikovsky smiling
> in gingerbread violins. I had yet to see myself
> as in a body too short and square for grace

"Anatomy is destiny," the speaker realizes. The body always fails. Yet what drives the speaker to keep pushing past the limits of physicality is the ardent need for perfection, an obsessive need for control. Holding onto that is the speaker's totem of security. If pain can be mastered, if trauma can be suppressed and memories forgotten, can life itself be controlled?

But the folly in chasing perfection is that it is inherently an unattainable goal: "I was doomed to an unrequited love / of this art."

> All my life I wanted to be versatile
> in every limb, my spinning heart
> and poses bowed and curved.
> My cymbaled vaults crossed
> the wooden floors in long leaps.
> But time aloft was always followed
> by hard landings.

When the speaker crosses the stage and leaps there is a moment, however fleeting, of perfection. One single transcendent moment of forgetting. That stretch of time encompasses a psychological breadth of space and relatively in which all things are possible. So great is the distraction of flight that joy itself can be its own reward.

But time resumes and the moment cannot last. Life continues. The crash inevitably comes. The fall is a terror. Peace is just out of reach. Elegant fantasy is disrupted mid-flight when feathers are dropped and "stopped midair, / me the weight of births, / marriages, and deaths." A pattern of absence, loss, and yearning ensues. The weight of traumas hang like stones.

And yet getting up to try and fail again is better than to exist in a perpetual morass of anguish, loneliness, and depression. Because now there is new memory of freedom:

> It's the dark
> season now, and so good
> to think of light. To know a new solstice
> awaits. And we turn, as into an open door.

The only way to experience euphoria is by first knowing intimate pain. Pain makes the appreciation of living ever more sweeter. Recovering from trauma isn't about denying the past and running away from it, but by embracing it instead and remembering lessons learnt. An innate sense of worth is upheld by newfound wisdom—you are resilient, you are independent, you can survive. It's a conviction hard-earned and only knowable through pain.

Ballet embodies the euphoria of being uplifted in the air before the inevitable crash down. But knowing you can survive this is what lets you get back up and try to take flight once more. Not even the death of a loved one can extinguish such hope:

> Now that your last breath has been taken
> and you're free of the heavy work
> of dying, I think of your splendid leap
> out of that hard start. How you lofted
> into recovery from addiction
> and on your spread wings
> lifted hundreds of others
> who came to bear witness of this.

Arabesque is a depiction of survival and renewal. It is an embodiment of "The grace of swan wings." It's a lightness in being.

THE PRACTICING POET
by Diane Lockward

REVIEWED BY ELIZABETH NICHOLS, CA

Diane Lockward describes *The Practicing Poet: Writing Beyond the Basics* as a "craft book," and on the back cover adds the subtitle "Poems, prompts, Tips, and Essays on Craft." Lockward's emphasis on "the craft of poetry" underscores the processes and the methods of writing poetry. Like Lockward's other craft books—*The Crafty Poet: Portable Workshop* and *The Crafty Poet II: A Portable Workshop*, *The Practicing Poet* is organized into ten parts, each devoted to a poetic concept. The ten sections are as follows: "Discovering New Material," "Finding the Best Words," "Making Music," "Working With Sentences and Line Breaks," "Crafting Surprise," "Achieving Tone," "Dealing With Feelings," "Transforming Your Poems," "Rethinking and Revising," and "Publishing Your Book." Each "Craft Tip" is written by one of over twenty accomplished poets. As editor, Lockward guides the practicing poet from the beginnings and crafting of a poem to the finish line of publishing that poem. Lockward advises the reader that the book is "geared toward the practicing poet who already has knowledge of the basic skills" and is designed to push "poets beyond the basics." In addition, Lockward introduces a new feature in this craft book: a Top Tips list. The Top Tips list features prominent poets' lists of their best pieces of poetry wisdom. With this new feature Lockward lets the reader feel like they are in conversation with other practicing poets, creating a sort of contemporary forum for the craft of poetry. As such, Lockward envisions *The Practicing Poet: Writing Beyond the Basics* as a useful tool in classrooms, workshops, and on the shelves of independent poets.

The first five sections of the book delve into different poetic techniques to craft impactful poems. To this end, poet Sandy Longhorn advises that the practicing poet employ various writing exercises to spark inspiration, such as word banks, columns of words, freewrites, journaling, and collecting phrases. Poet Natasha Sajé advocates researching different topics and the etymology of words to inspire and flesh out poems. On etymology in particular, Sajé elucidates, "The etymology of a word can deepen the meaning of a poem by carrying an image." Throughout the book, these accomplished poets cannot help but surround their craft tips with metaphor, simile, personification, and imagery. For example, Sajé concludes her section on the utility of etymology to the craft of poetry by saying, "Poems must, of course, be well made; no one likes to sit in a chair that wobbles. Using the history of words can strengthen that chair, giving it roots." Accordingly, in the third and fourth sections, poets Marge Piercy and Molly Peacock highlight the use onomatopoeia, repetition, anaphora, alliteration, assonance, rhyme, and syntax. Even the structure of language, instructs Piercy in "Craft Tip #7," can affect the music of a poem; exclamations, commands, questions, fragments, compound and complex sentences can all impact the way a poem sounds. The first five sections of the book, then, lay the groundwork for more complex exercises to help improve a poet's craft.

The next four sections in *The Practicing Poet* address more advanced methods to hone the craft of poetry. Section V, "Crafting Surprise," discusses different ways a poet might engender a sense of surprise and discovery in his or her work. Poet Meg Day, for example, lists line breaks, slant truth, and unconscious or instinctual writing as avenues to surprise in poetry. Section VI, "Achieving Tone" follows the breadcrumbs of the previous section by exploring tone, particularly the unique voice of the poet. "We need to make deliberate gestures," Peter E. Murphy states, "that reveal our inner nurturer or our inner freak and our inner blue blood. We need to experiment with words and phrases so our poems sound more like our inner us, unique and uniquely crafted." After all, Adrian Blevins adds later, "How we feel about our speakers is even more important in poetry." This advice flows easily into the next section, "Dealing with Feelings," which considers the effect of sentimentality on a poem. The danger in expressing feelings, Patrick Donnelly explains, is "too much sweetness or melodrama." Salves to the danger of melodrama, according to Donnelly, include acerbity, coldness, danger, and vulnerability. Finally, sections VIII and IX explore tips for "Transforming Your Poems" and "Rethinking and Revising" poems, respectively. Transformation occurs—a la poets Sharon Bryan, Jennifer Givhan, and Traci Brimhall—by playing with point of view, magical realism, and word choice. And revision, declares Campbell McGrath, "is the real work of the poet;" it is a necessary part of the craft of poetry that can "erase the poem down to its…core" and ultimately rebuild it into a stronger work.

"Publishing Your Book"—the last section in The Practicing Poet—is perhaps the most useful to advanced poetry crafters. As April Ossmann puts it, manuscript order alone can "the biggest mystery to emerging and sometimes established poets." Unique to Ossmann's recommendations in the ordering of a poetry manuscript is her admittance that, "I don't often recommend titling sections, because it is often feels too telling, directive, or limiting of potential interpretations.... Titling sections for such manuscripts works best when it heightens ambiguities or adds potential rather than explains." Ossmann's conversational tone in this section helps to demystify the process of manuscript order. In addition, Adele Kenny has tips for "Protocol at Poetry Readings" to make a good, enhanced impact with one's work at a poetry reading. As an experienced poet and director of the long-running Carriage House Poetry Series, practicing poets are well-served with Kenny's tips in this regard.

The one tip in section ten and in the whole of *The Practicing Poet* that falls short is "Craft Tip #29: The Work of Promoting Your Poetry Book." It is true, as Lockward explains, that many poets find themselves doing a large part of promotion on their own. However, I question Lockward's assertion that "the email blitz is the single most important thing you can do to get your book off to a good start." I posit that the most important thing a contemporary poet can do vis-a-vis self-promotion is to build a social media following. Lockward references social media, but lists it—in order of importance—after the email blitz, personal website, launch party, and reading. A poet actively promoting their work is better served building a presence on social media even before the promotion of their manuscript. In this way, the poet knows that he or she has an excited, captivated audience ready to read and share the new work. 21st century students—and adults for that matter—read email because they have to: they go on social media because they want to. Of course, the "email blitz," personal website, launch party, and reading are still all useful tools to keep in a poet's "promotion toolbox" and, when they work in tandem, can yield results.

In teaching the practicing poet the craft of poetry, the accomplished poets that masthead each "Craft Tip" also reveal what they think about poetry: what they feel poetry is and is not. What makes a good poem good, and a lackluster poem not-so-good. This is, perhaps, the most illuminating aspect of *The Practicing Poet: Writing Beyond the Basics* to the experienced poet trying to hone his or her craft. Writers learn best from other writers; so, too, poets from other poets. It is in this respect that casual readers and m practicing poets will find *The Practicing Poet* a valuable resource for the craft of poetry.

NARROW BRIDGE
by Robbi Nester

Reviewed by Linda E. Kim

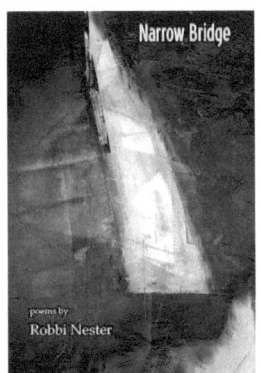

In Robbi Nester's *Narrow Bridge*, characters are deeply in tune with nature. But it is when they become disassociated from the natural world that they become detached, hardened, and numb. This alienation is depicted as unnatural because identity becomes lost. Humans end up distracted from the things that truly matter in a world of manufactured things, which are finite in form and possibility. So the speaker seeks ways in which the artificial and the natural can reconcile and interact harmoniously.

The respect given to biomes and creatures is seen in the reverence the speaker has for the world and its environs. Imagery is wondrous, stunning, preciously cradled in the observer's gentle hands. Lines of beauty engage the senses. Diction and language are whimsical.

Joy is found in the water bear, the tarantula, the crab. King snakes, cicadas, and minnows can be found occupying the land, the skies, the seas. But the speaker argues humans can occupy those spaces just as harmoniously. Natural phenomena are imbued with the qualities of living things: "The waves / extend their white fingers" and "The sea spreads her lacy / petticoats wide on the dunes..." It is a metamorphosis both beautiful and malleable. Boundaries are made seamless. The human form becoming entwined with the natural world demonstrates harmony between the two.

Birds are particularly highlighted as extraordinary. Their flight embodies freedom. They have an effortless sense of direction. They can find their way with grace and adaptability:

> The green and blue labyrinth below
> smooths to a map, a magnetic grid
> no human can perceive without
> the aid of compass or GPS.

Yet the sharp contrast made between bird and human highlights a tension. The manmade is shown to be finite and limited. Natural instinct is shown to be so much more effective than society's poor imitations. In this duality there is a suggestion that humans have lost their way, that the artificial can be distracting. But the speaker sees a way to reconcile the two worlds. She closes the distance between the two.

In the poem "Imaginary Chef," manmade and natural spaces easily meld together:

> In my kitchen, gleaming copper saucepans wink,
> my mise-en-place a thing of wonder,
> the cupboards perfectly arranged.
> I taste the world, scenting ripeness
>
> ...
>
> I am master of every ingredient.
> The earth's simplest offerings,
> onions, potatoes, garlic,
> sweetened for weeks beneath the earth,
> yield up their savor to my sauce,
> its splash of cream spreading
> like a cloud on a blue ceramic sky.

Imagination effortlessly transforms a "splash of cream" into an imaginative cloud floating on "a blue ceramic sky." The kitchen is made into a liminal space through the speaker's mind. It is a space of contemplation and reflection. The playfulness of the language shows a deep appreciation for cooking, but there is also a profound wisdom behind the acknowledgment that "the simple act of nourishment" is due to a life-giving earth.

The speaker clearly advocates for cherishing the earth. In this, flexible thinking is required. Appreciating and taking care of our environment brings us closer to our natural selves, to who we are meant to be. It is the speaker's way of negotiating humanity's distance from nature.

Instead of mastering nature and further skewing the power imbalance, the speaker instead shows how coexistence is possible. Harmony can inspire and open up new possibilities:

> The world is my palette,
> colors and shades of taste
> capable of endless combination

The fluidity of the poetry suggests that just as nature is flexible and adaptable so too are human beings. When people take on such qualities, it gives them the resiliency needed to tackle life.

"At the Root" teases at such possibilities:

> Under the damp earth, taking sustenance
> from the dark, white icicles of daikon,
> multi-colored carrots, potatoes in all sizes,
> perfect globes and tubers. What can we
> learn from roots that might
> inform our lives?

At the core of identity is the question of how to define ourselves. But we can chafe inside boundaries determined by others, so solitude serves as a comfort. Mental escapism becomes a key coping skill. Imaginative preoccupation sustains the speaker. When family conflict controls the spaces around you, occupying the domestic sphere can become ill fitting and wholly unwelcome.

Growing up is a delicate period in which a child has to learn how to navigate, occupy, and negotiate manmade spaces, especially those spaces as dictated by others. Having no control over your own environment spurs helplessness. In childhood the speaker acutely feels this lack of agency. Huddling in tight, small spaces in order to hide is the only way to flee "my father's rages, / my mother's expectations."

Comfort can only be sought by hiding in the dark or by mentally retreating:

> I would huddle on the crooked stairs,
> flashlight in hand, and read for hours
> or sit astride the stationary bike
> pretending to be soaring among clouds.

But as the speaker is forced to grow up, several traumas are suffered. Familial bonds are not nurturing. Religion proves alienating. And a society that pursues power engenders systematic corruption. In the face of weaponry and war, birds have "long since blown out of the sky." People are divorced from their own humanity. It is little wonder that the speaker seeks comfort in imaginative things. It is little wonder that it seems safer to shut others out.

However, solitude too easily becomes isolation. The bridge is the focal point of connection. It embodies the literal and metaphorical distance between people. It is only when they decide to no longer cross that understanding becomes lost. Manmade barriers prevent empathy and only reinforce inhuman separation.

But the answer to reconciliation and healing can be found in "Season of Mending:"

> All my life, I've left a trail of broken things—
> first mangled toys, lost game pieces, missing
> cards, then bungled knitting, fallen
> cakes, buttons that won't
> stay sewn. Relationships as well
> break down: harsh words can't
> be unsaid; candor cools lifelong alliances.
> At first, I never tried to fix such breaks,
> just moved on, hoping for better luck.
> Now, buried in the drifts of what
> I've left behind, I turn to mending

The speaker realizes how to reconcile with an artificial world that only destroys. Through the painstaking work of mending relationships, it is possible to see new paths. The bridge is narrow, but it is possible to overcome its limitations with the help of others.

It is not easy, however. "Ties" demonstrates the sheer absurdity of how difficult it is to bridge the gap between human beings:

> Now I hear that chemists have discovered
> how to knot a strand of molecules
> "only 20 nanometres long," according
> to the source I read. This "octoknot"
> defeats all efforts to untie its bond.

> We've grown so skilled at linking the invisible,
>
> and yet connections in the larger world
> elude us. Perhaps their very size
> makes manifest the differences we fear,
> as magnifying mirrors make the ordinary strange.

Empathy is key. By focusing on the things that connect us, we can move away from the barriers that divide us. Even if the world we inhabit is one that encourages anything but connectivity, we must still try. Reaching out to others to create ties is the only way to widen that narrow bridge of understanding:

> Taxonomists of difference, we're distracted
> by the obvious distinctions. So I practice
> knotting this to that, finding likeness
> where it never was before

Instead of obsessively despairing over inhuman separations, the speaker chooses to revel in the profoundity of nature, of life. Out of destruction and trauma there is the possibility of growth.

In "Out of Season," the speaker dreams of spring: "In early fall, I dream of trees / in full blossom." These "tiny identical blooms" are sparks of brightness amidst life's travails.

In living things there is hope. Dreaming can be done only in defiance of despair. In an act that epitomizes hope, we reach out to others out of desire for lightness instead of stagnation.

PUBLICATION CREDITS

Shanta Acharya: "Coconut Milk" was featured in *Imagine: New and Selected Poems by Shanta Acharya*, published by HarperCollins Publishers, India, 2017.

Cynthia Gallaher: The poem "May You Have Salty Days Ahead" previously appeared in both *Epicurean Ecstasy: More Poems About Food, Drink, Herbs and Spices* (The Poetry Box, Portland, 2019), and *Drenched* (Main Street Rag, Charlotte, N.C., 2018).

Jane Hirshfield: "*Da Capo,*" "Milk," and "Wine Grapes for Breakfast" are from *The Lives of the Heart* © 1997 Jane Hirshfield (NY: HarperCollins), used by permission of the author, all rights reserved.

Jeannie E. Roberts: "Oyster" previously appeared in *The Poeming Pigeon, A Literary Journal of Poetry: Poems About Food* and *Romp and Ceremony* (Finishing Line Press, 2017).

Contributor Notes

Born and brought up in India, **Shanta Acharya** was among the first batch of women admitted to Worcester College, Oxford, where she was awarded the Doctor of Philosophy for her work on Ralph Waldo Emerson. She was a Visiting Scholar in the Department of English and American Literature and Languages at Harvard University before joining an American investment bank in London, where she lives. The author of eleven books, her publications range from poetry, literary criticism and fiction to finance. *Imagine: New and Selected Poems by Shanta Acharya* appeared in 2017. www.shantaacharya.com

Rita Anderson is a poet and playwright from Austin, Texas. Her work is told from a female point-of-view and a working-class background. Anderson is the Dramatists Guild Regional Representative (Austin/San Antonio), is on the Social Media Team for the International Center for Women Playwrights (ICWP), and is faculty at Interlochen. Anderson has an MFA in Poetry and an MA in Playwriting, and she's a member of Poets & Writers and The Academy of American Poets. Anderson was poetry editor of *ELLIPSIS*, the literary journal at University of New Orleans, and both of her poetry books— *The Entropy of Rocketman* (Finishing Line Press,) and *Watched Pots (A Lovesong to Motherhood)*—have been nominated for the Pushcart Prize. Her poetry has won several awards, including one from the Academy of American Poets, and Anderson's work has appeared in over 100 literary publications, including *Spoon River Poetry Review,* and the upcoming anthologies, *Waves: A Confluence of Voices* (an anthology from A Room of One's Own AROHO Foundation), and *Endlessly Rocking (An Anthology to Celebrate Walt Whitman's 200th Birthday)*. Contact Anderson at her website www.rita-anderson.com

Ruth Bavetta's poems have appeared in *Rattle, North American Review, Nimrod, Rhino, Tar River Review, Slant, Atlanta Review* and many others, and are included in several anthologies. Her books include *Fugitive Pigments*, and *Flour, Water, Salt* (FutureCycle), *Embers on the Stairs* (Moontide), and *No Longer at This Address* (Aldrich). She loves the light of November afternoons, the music of Stravinsky, and the smell of the ocean. She hates pretense, fundamentalism and sauerkraut.

Daisy Bassen is a poet and practicing physician who graduated magna cum laude from Princeton University's Creative Writing Program and completed her medical training at The University of Rochester and Brown. Her work has been published in *Oberon*, *The Delmarva Review*, *The Sow's Ear*, and *Tuck Magazine* as well as multiple other journals. She was a semi-finalist in the 2016 Vassar Miller Prize in Poetry, a finalist in the 2018 Adelaide Literary Prize, and the winner of the So to Speak 2019 Poetry Contest. She was nominated for the 2019 *Best of the Net Anthology* and was doubly nominated for a 2019 Pushcart Prize. She lives in Rhode Island with her family.

Margo Berdeshevsky, born in New York city, often lives and writes now in Paris. Her latest poetry collection, *Before The Drought,* is from Glass Lyre Press, (2017.) (In an early version, it was finalist for the National Poetry Series.) Berdeshevsky is also the author of *Between Soul & Stone* and *But a Passage in Wilderness* (Sheep Meadow Press). Her book of illustrated stories, *Beautiful Soon Enough,* received the first Ronald Sukenick Innovative Fiction Award for Fiction Collective Two (University of Alabama Press). Other honors include the Robert H. Winner Award from the Poetry Society of America, a portfolio of her poems in the *Aeolian Harp Series, Volume 1* (Glass Lyre Press), the *& Now Anthology of the Best of Innovative Writing,* and numerous Pushcart prize nominations. Her works appear in: *Poetry International, New Letters, Kenyon Review, Plume, The Collagist, Tupelo Quarterly, Gulf Coast, Southern Humanities Review, Pleiades, Prairie Schooner, The American Journal of Poetry, Jacar—One, Mānoa, Pirene's Fountain, Big Other,* and many others. In Europe her works have been seen in *The Poetry Review* (UK) *The Wolf, Europe, Siècle 21, & Confluences Poétiques, Recours au Poème,* and *Levure Littéraire.* A multi-genre hybrid book, *Square Black Key* and a new poetry collection, *It Is Still Beautiful To Hear The Heart Beat,* wait at the gate. She may be found reading from her books in London, Paris, New York City, Los Angeles, Honolulu, or somewhere new in the world. Her "Letters from Paris" may be found in Poetry International at https://poetryinternationalonline.com/category/letters/letters-from-paris/ … For more information, kindly see http://margoberdeshevsky.com

J. P. Dancing Bear is editor for the *Verse Daily* and Dream Horse Press. He is the author of fourteen collections of poetry, most recently *Cephalopodic* (Glass Lyre Press, 2015). His most recent book, *Fish Singing Foxes* came out in March of 2019 (Salmon Poetry). His next collection, *Of Oracles and Monsters*, will be released by Glass Lyre Press in the fall of 2019. His work has appeared in hundreds of magazines and anthologies, including *American Literary Review, Crazyhorse, Plume, Quarterly West* and others.

Yoko Danno is Japanese and writes poetry solely in English. Her poems have appeared in various international poetry journals and anthologies online and in print. Her recent poetry books are *Aquamarine* (Glass Lyre Press, 2014), *Woman in a Blue Robe* (Isobar Press, 2016) and *Further Center* (Ikuta Press, 2017). *The Songs and Stories of the Kojiki* a collection of creation myths, songs and historical narratives compiled in eighth-century Japan was published by Ahadada Books in 2008 and the revised 2nd version by Red Moon Press in 2014. *Photo Scrolls,* a collection of experimental prose poems with photos in collaboration with James C. Hopkins, is forthcoming early next year. She lives in Kobe, Japan.

Lori Desrosiers' poetry books are *The Philosopher's Daughter,* (Salmon Poetry , 2013) and *Sometimes I Hear the Clock Speak* (Salmon Poetry, 2016). A third full-length book, *Keeping Planes in the Air,* will be released by Salmon Poetry in 2020. Two more chapbooks, *Inner Sky* and *typing with e.e. cummings,* are from Glass Lyre Press, 2015 and 2019. Her poems have appeared in *New Millennium Review, Cutthroat, Peacock Journal, String Poet, Blue Fifth Review, Pirene's Fountain, New Verse News, Mom Egg Review,* and many other journals and anthologies. She was a finalist for the Joy Harjo poetry contest and the New Millennium contest. Her poem "about the body" won the Liakoura poetry award from Glass Lyre Press. She holds an MFA in Poetry from New England College. Her work has been nominated for a Pushcart Prize. She founded and edits *Naugatuck River Review,* a journal of narrative poetry, and *Wordpeace.co,* an online journal dedicated to social justice. She teaches Poetry in the Interdisciplinary Studies program for the Lesley University M.F.A. graduate program. Her website is http://loridesrosierspoetry.com.

Alicia Elkort's poetry has been published in *AGNI, Arsenic Lobster, Black Lawrence Press, Georgia Review, Heron Tree, The Hunger Journal, Jet Fuel Review,*

Menacing Hedge, Rogue Agent, Stirring: A Literary Collection, Tinderbox Poetry Journal, and many others. Her poems have been nominated for the Orisons Anthology (2016), the Pushcart (2017), and a Best of the Net (2018). Alicia reads for *Tinderbox Poetry Journal,* mostly with a cup of strong black tea in hand.

Susan Fox's poems have appeared in dozens of journals and anthologies, from *Poetry, The Paris Review,* and *The New York Quarterly* to *The New York Times,* and the Glass Lyre Press anthology *Collateral Damage.* She was born in Ohio and has lived in New York (where she taught English Literature in the City University), Rome, Paris, and rural Normandy. She has published literary criticism and travel journalism. An opera to her original full-length libretto about a hidden child in World War II had its semi-professional premiere in New York, and her screenplay of another Holocaust story was optioned for film. She lives in Manhattan with her husband, physicist Steve Orenstein.

Diane Frank is author of seven books of poems, two novels, and a photo memoir of her 400 mile trek in the Nepal Himalayas, *Letters from a Sacred Mountain Place.* Her new book of poems, *Canon for Bears and Ponderosa Pines,* was published by Glass Lyre Press and received honors in the San Francisco Book Festival. *Blackberries in the Dream House,* her first novel, won the Chelson Award for Fiction and was nominated for the Pulitzer Prize. Diane lives in San Rafael, where she dances, plays cello, and creates her life as an art form. She performs with the Golden Gate Symphony in San Francisco. www.dianefrank.net

Cynthia Gallaher, a Chicago-based poet, is author of four poetry collections, including *Epicurean Ecstasy: More Poems About Food, Drink, Herbs and Spices* (The Poetry Box, Portland, 2019), and three chapbooks, including *Drenched* (Main Street Rag, Charlotte, N.C., 2018). The Chicago Public Library lists her among its "Top Ten Requested Chicago Poets."

Jane Hirshfield's ninth book of poetry, *Ledger,* will appear from Knopf in March 2020. A former chancellor of the Academy of American Poets and newly elected to the American Academy of Arts & Sciences, Hirshfield's poems appear in *The New Yorker, The Atlantic, The New York Review of Books, Poetry,* and ten volumes of *The Best American Poetry.* She has a special interest in working at the intersection of art, science, and the issues of biosphere and social justice.

Carol Levin is the author of three full collections: *An Undercurrent of Jitters* (MoonPath Press 2018), *Confident Music Would Fly Us to Paradise* (MoonPath

Press, 2014), and *Stunned By the Velocity* (Pecan Grove Press, 2012.) She is also the author of the chapbooks *Red Rooms and Others* (Pecan Grove, Press 2009), and *Sea Lions Sing Scat* (Finishing Line Press, 2007). Her work has been published in journals and anthologies, print and online, in Russia, New Zealand, Germany and the US. As a founding member and Literary Manager of The Art Theatre of Puget Sound, she, along with two Russians, translated Chekhov's four major plays. She is an Editorial Assistant at *Crab Creek Review* and has recent or forthcoming work in *Literary Accents, The Main Street Rag, The Cape Rock, Women Arts Quarterly Review* and *The Poetry Box.*

Cameron Morse lives with his wife Lili and son Theodore in Blue Springs, Missouri. He was diagnosed with a glioblastoma in 2014. With a 14.6 month life expectancy, he entered the Creative Writing program at the University of Missouri, Kansas City and, in 2018, graduated with an M.F.A. His poems have been published in numerous magazines, including *New Letters, Bridge Eight,* and *South Dakota Review.* His first collection, *Fall Risk,* won Glass Lyre Press's 2018 Best Book Award. His second, *Father Me Again,* is available from Spartan Press and chapbook *Coming Home with Cancer* is forthcoming in Blue Lyra Press's Delphi Poetry Series. For more information, check out his Facebook page or website.

Robbi Nester is the author of four books of poetry, chapbook *Balance* (White Violet, 2012) and three collections, the most recent of which is *Narrow Bridge* (Main Street Rag, 2019). She has also edited two anthologies of poetry: *The Liberal Media Made Me Do It!* (Nine Toes, 2014) and an Ekphrastic e-book published as a special issue of Poemeleon Poetry Journal, *Over the Moon: Birds, Beasts, and Trees—Celebrating the Photography of Beth Moon.* Her poems, reviews, essays, and articles have appeared widely, most recently in *Praxis, Tiferet, London Review, Visual Verse, Writing in a Woman's Voice, Sheila-na-Gig, RHINO,* and the anthologies *Dark Ink, Collateral Damage,* and *Poets Facing the Wall.* She also has a chapbook of chef poems, *Plated,* that will be looking for a home soon.

Joey Nicoletti is the author of eight books and chapbooks, including *Boombox Serenade,* which is forthcoming this winter, and *Cannoli Gangster,* his first full-length poetry collection, which was a finalist for the 2009 Steel Toe

Books Prize. A former poetry editor of *Sou'wester*, Nicoletti currently teaches at SUNY Buffalo State.

Connie Post served as the first Poet Laureate of Livermore from 2005 to 2009. During that time she wrote over twenty five poems of occasion for civic events. She also created two popular reading series. Post's poems appear widely in magazines such as *Calyx, Dogwood, Blue Fifth Review, Two Bridges Review, Comstock Review, Spoon River Poetry Review, River Styx, Crab Creek Review, Slipstream, The Big Muddy, Slippery Elm, Valparaiso Poetry Review* and *Verse Daily*. Her first full length collection *Floodwater* was published in 2014 by Glass Lyre Press and won the Lyrebird Award. Her chapbook *And When the Sun Drops* won the 2012 Aurorean Editor's chapbook prize. Her work has appeared in several anthologies, including *Alongside we Travel – Contemporary Poets on Autism* (NYQ Books, 2019), *Collateral Damage* (Glass Lyre Press), *Carrying the Branch* (Glass Lyre Press) and *Truth to Power: Writers Respond To The Rhetoric Of Hate And Fear* (Cutthroat Magazine). Her poetry awards include the 2018 Liakoura Award, the *Crab Creek Review* Poetry Award, the Caesura Award and the Prick of the Spindle Poetry Competition. In addition, she won second place for the Jack Kerouac Poetry Prize and the Atticus Review Poetry Prize.

Jeannie E. Roberts is the author of six books, including *The Wingspan of Things* (Dancing Girl Press, 2017), *Romp and Ceremony* (Finishing Line Press, 2017), *Beyond Bulrush* (Lit Fest Press, 2015), and *Nature of it All* (Finishing Line Press, 2013). She is also author and illustrator of *Rhyme the Roost! A Collection of Poems and Paintings for Children* (Daffydowndilly Press, an imprint of Kelsay Books, 2019) and *Let's Make Faces!* (author-published, 2009). Her work appears in print and online in North American and international journals and anthologies. She holds a B.S. in secondary education, M.A. in arts and cultural management, and is poetry editor of the online literary magazine *Halfway Down the Stairs*. When she's not reading, writing, or editing, you can find her drawing and painting, or outdoors photographing her natural surroundings.

Claire D. Roof is an assistant professor of English at Ivy Tech Community College in South Bend, Indiana. She was the editor of the school's creative journal, the *Ivy Quill*, for six editions. She has recently published poems in the

Common Ground Review, *MockingHeart Review*, and *Pirene's Fountain* Tenth Anniversary Issue. She will have two poems coming out in *Flint Hills Review*.

Claudia Serea's poems and translations have been published in *Field, New Letters, Prairie Schooner, The Malahat Review, Oxford Poetry, Asymptote, Gravel*, and elsewhere. She is the author of five poetry collections, most recently *Twoxism*, a collaboration with visual artist Maria Haro (8th House Publishing, 2018), and *Nothing Important Happened Today* (Broadstone Books, 2016). Serea's poem "My Father's Quiet Friends in Prison, 1958-1962" received the 2013 *New Letters* Readers Award. She won the *2014 Levure Littéraire* Award for Poetry Performance, the 2006 New Women's Voices competition, and several honorable mentions for her poems and books. Serea is a founding editor of *National Translation Month*, and co-hosts The Williams Poetry Readings in Rutherford, NJ.

Neil Silberblatt's poems have appeared, or will be appearing shortly, in numerous journals, including *The American Journal of Poetry, Tikkun Daily, Plume Poetry Journal, The Aurorean, Mom Egg Review, Ibbetson Street Press, Naugatuck River Review, Chantarelle's Notebook, Canopic Jar, Muddy River Poetry Review, Nixes Mate Review, Verse Daily*, and *The Good Men Project*. His poem, "Burnt Offering," was selected by Mass Poetry as their "Poem of the Moment." He has published two poetry collections: *So Far, So Good* (2012) and *Present Tense* (2013), and has been nominated for a Pushcart Prize. His most recent poetry book, *Past Imperfect* (Nixes Mate Books, 2018), was nominated for the Mass Book Award in Poetry.

Neil is the founder/director of Voices of Poetry which has organized and presented a series of (more than 300) poetry events, featuring acclaimed poets—including Poets Laureate of Connecticut, Rhode Island, Vermont & New Hampshire—at various venues in NY, NJ, CT and MA; past venues include The Mount/Edith Wharton's home in Lenox, MA, the Provincetown Art Association & Museum, and The Rubin Museum of Art in NYC. Since 2014, Neil has also been the host of the *Poet's Corner* program on WOMR/WFMR out of Provincetown, for which he has interviewed accomplished and aspiring poets and writers on and off Cape Cod.

Kalpna Singh-Chitnis is an Indian-American poet and filmmaker. She is the author of four poetry collections and Editor-in-Chief of *Life and Legends*. Her work has appeared in notable journals like *World Literature Today, California Quarterly, Indian Literature, Pirene's Fountain* and others. Her poetry has been translated into many languages. Kalpna Singh-Chitnis participated in the "Silk Routes" project of the International Writing Program at the University of Iowa from 2014-2016. She has also been invited as a poet and panelist to speak at platforms like Sahitya Akademi (India's highest academy of letters,) AWP, and several international film festivals. Her awards and honors include - Naji Naaman Literary Prize for Creativity (2017), the Rajiv Gandhi Global Excellence Award for Cinema and Literature (2014), the title of Bihar Shri (1988) and the Bihar Rajbhasha Award (given by the government of Bihar, India) (1987). www.kalpnasinghchitnis.com

Tim Suermondt is the author of five full-length collections of poems; the latest is *Josephine Baker Swimming Pool* from MadHat Press, 2019. He has published in *Poetry, Ploughshares, Prairie Schooner, The Georgia Review, Bellevue Literary Review, Stand Magazine, Galway Review*, and *Plume* among many others. He lives in Cambridge, MA, with his wife, the poet Pui Ying Wong.

Maria Terrone is the author of the poetry collections *Eye to Eye* (Bordighera Press), *A Secret Room in Fall* (McGovern Prize, Ashland Poetry Press), and *The Bodies We Were Loaned* and a chapbook, *American Gothic, Take 2*. Her work, nominated four times for a Pushcart Prize has appeared in numerous media including *Poetry, Ploughshares, The Hudson Review* and *Poetry Daily*, and more than 25 anthologies. Since 2015, she has been poetry editor of the journal *Italian Americana*. Bordighera Press published *At Home in the New World*, her first collection of creative nonfiction, in 2018. www.mariaterrone.com

The Aeolian Harp Series, Volume 5

GUEST EDITOR
JOHN AMEN OF *PEDESTAL*

Featuring
Maura Alia Badji
Wendy Barker
Patrice Boyer Claeys
Peggy Dobreer
Amy Friedman
Dawn Manning
Cameron Morse
Lindsey Royce
Shikhandin
Ann Wehrman

Available Now!

Linda Blaskey's exquisite debut collection of poems is available as softcover and ebook from all major online retailers

White Horses is an extraordinary debut collection, rich in imagery and compassion, from poet Linda Blaskey, whose work was selected by Paterson Prize-winning poet Dorianne Laux for publication in the widely acclaimed Best New Poets anthology series. Mojave River Press is proud to present Linda Blaskey's brave collection of memory, love, loss, and nature, which poet Jan Beatty, winner of the Agnes Lynch Starrett Poetry Prize, describes as "exquisitely sensual, yet peaceful...a stunning book" and Pushcart Prize-winning poet Gerry LaFemina says is revelatory of "turmoil and ecstasy that roil beneath the tranquil surface." These poems will enchant and disarm. As Stephen Scott Whitaker of the National Book Critics Circle says about this remarkable first book, "These poems run wild with life."

In White Horses, *Linda Blaskey bravely writes moving poems filled with longing and loss. Hers is a voice exquisitely sensual, yet peaceful. These poems of trucks, back roads, family, and country breathe the ways of love, never treading into the sentimental. Blaskey writes of a life lived, the cost of work, of taking care of others—yet she never forgets the thrill of escape. A stunning book.*

—**Jan Beatty**, author of *Jackknife: New and Selected Poems*

With a kiss let us set out for an unknown world. —Alfred de Musset

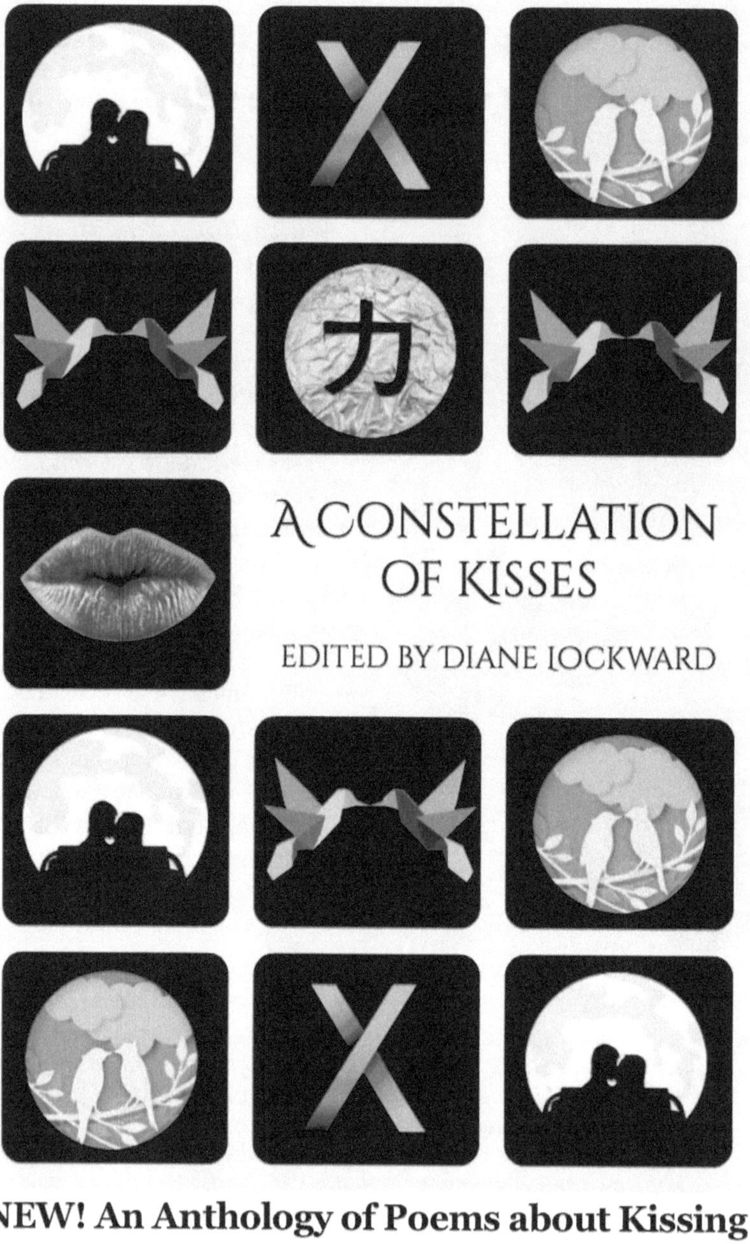

A CONSTELLATION OF KISSES

EDITED BY DIANE LOCKWARD

NEW! An Anthology of Poems about Kissing

107 poems by such poets as David Kirby, Kim Addonizio, Ellen Bass, Dorianne Laux, and Richard Jones

Terrapin Books
www.terrapinbooks.com
ISBN: 978-1947896178
$18.99   202 pages
Available from Amazon, B&N, and wherever books are sold

The Practicing Poet

Writing Beyond the Basics

edited by

Diane Lockward

NEW! A craft book for poets

Includes craft tips, model poems, prompts, top tips lists.
Contributors are 113 of today's most accomplished poets, such as Jan
Beatty, Maggie Smith, George Bilgere, Patricia Smith, Robert Wrigley.
Appropritate for the classroom or workshop or at home.

Terrapin Books
www.terrapinbooks.com
ISBN: 978-1-947896-07-9
$21.00 / 350 pages
Available from Amazon, B&N, and wherever books are sold

BEFORE THE DROUGHT

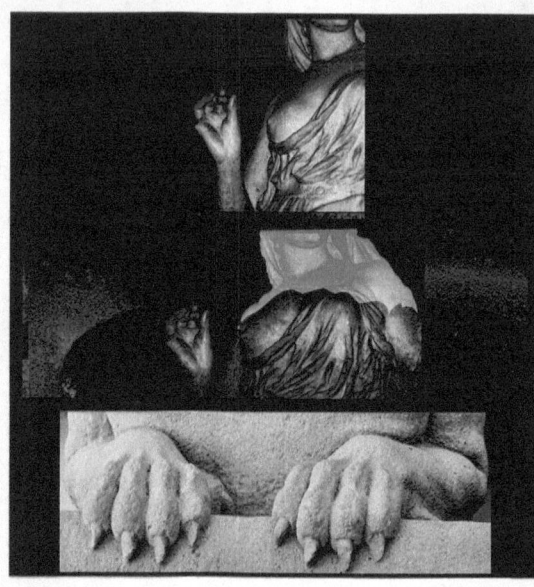

MARGO BERDESHEVSKY

FROM GLASS LYRE PRESS

https://tinyurl.com/yblnd28y

In the City of Light, Berdeshevsky writes poems commensurate with her vision, poems that know to ask *How close is death, how near is God?* Hers is a book to read at the precipice on which we stand.   — Carolyn Forché

MARGO BERDESHEVSKY

http://margoberdeshevsky/com

"In this new and startling collection, Diane Frank's poems transcend not just genres but entire dimensions. When she speaks to J.S. Bach, she really means it and when Bach speaks back, she listens — entirely — the way certain moths perceive sound via their whole body, even their wings. How is this accomplished? It will seem to come through the poems themselves — their music, tonal qualities and subjects, yet it goes even deeper as it pushes up like duende through the soles of your feet. The voice is declarative, emphatic, spirit driven. She will tell you, 'When a buffalo enters your dream, / listen for arpeggio hooves, / the weight of music, / a copper moon / above a vanishing prairie' and you will, you must listen."

—**Lois P. Jones,** author of *Night Ladder*
Radio Host, KPFK's *Poets Café*

Order from Glass Lyre Press

https://glass-lyre-press.myshopify.com/collections/full-length-collections-1/products/canon-for-bears-and-ponderosa-pines

RHINO 2019

Publishing poetry,
flash fiction, & translations

With work from more than 120 poets, RHINO 2019 is our largest ever! See why *New Pages* writes of *RHINO*:

"It is poetry wrought from life, distilled over time into art...
We are all of these poems. They are talking to us."

See website for sample poems, submission guidelines, contest information, and to order new or back issues.

Order the 2019 issue online: $16 (plus s&h)

2020 issue submissions open: April 15 – July 31
2020 Founders' Prize Contest submissions: Sept. 1 – Oct. 15

Our online **RHINO Reviews!** features 8-10 new short reviews each month of the most compelling current releases in contemporary American poetry.

We've been in publication for **more than 40 years**, creating a vibrant and supportive community of writers and editors.

rhinopoetry.org

Glass Lyre Press

exceptional works to replenish the spirit

Glass Lyre Press is an independent literary publisher interested in technically accomplished, stylistically distinct, and original work. Glass Lyre seeks diverse writers that possess a dynamic aesthetic and an ability to emotionally and intellectually engage a wide audience of readers.

Glass Lyre's vision is to connect the world through language and art. We hope to expand the scope of poetry and short fiction for the general reader through exceptionally well-written books, which evoke emotion, provide insight, and resonate with the human spirit.

Poetry Collections
Poetry Chapbooks
Select Short & Flash Fiction
Anthologies

www.GlassLyrePress.com